Fighting Past Each Other
The New Zealand Wars 1845-1875

Matthew Wright

Author's note
This book is a companion to my adult volume, *Two peoples, One Land*, which has complete citations, bibliography and related evidence.

Published by Reed Children's Books, a division of Reed Publishing (NZ) Ltd, 39 Rawene Road, Birkenhead, Auckland 10. Associated companies, branches and representatives throughout the world.

This book is copyright. Except for the purposes of fair reviewing, no part of this publication may be reproduced or transmitted in any form or by any means, electronic or mechanical, including photocopying, recording, or any information storage and retrieval system, without permission in writing from the publisher. Infringers of copyright render themselves liable to prosecution.

© 2006 Matthew Wright
The author asserts his moral rights in the work.
© 2005 Suzy Brown — illustrations

A catalogue entry for this book is available from the National Library of New Zealand.

ISBN 10: 1 86948 424 X
ISBN 13: 978 1 86948 424 8
First published 2006

Edited by Carolyn Lagahetau
Designed by Jason Anscomb

Printed in China

CONTENTS

Introduction	5
Who fought the wars?	6
Why the wars started	7
War in the north, 1845–46	9
The Wellington war, 1846–47	12
The Taranaki war	15
The war for Waitara, March 1860–March 1861	16
The Waikato war	20
The war down the Waikato River, July 1863–January 1864	21
The legend of Rewi's last stand, March 1864	23
The battle of Gate Pa, March 1864	26
A different war, 1864–66	29
War on the East Coast, 1865–66	31
The battle of Omarunui, October 1866	32
Titokowaru's war, June 1868–April 1869	34
Te Kooti's escape, 1868–69	37
Matawhero and Ngatapa, November 1868–January 1869	39
Whakatane, Mohaka and the Urewera, April–May 1869	40
The Taupo campaign, 1869–70	42
The end of Te Kooti's war	44
Peace with the King Country, 1881–83	45
The war and historians	47
Selected further reading	47
Index	48

INTRODUCTION

The New Zealand wars began in 1845 and went on for nearly 30 years. They went on for so long that even when they had finished, nobody quite believed the fighting was over, and the government continued to build forts and pay soldiers to live in them.

The wars have been called by many names. Some call them the Maori Wars. At one time they were called the Land Wars. Still other historians have called them the Colonial Wars. But most often we call them the New Zealand Wars, which is probably the simplest and best term.

There was no single war. Fighting began in the Bay of Islands in 1845–47. There was another war in Wellington and the Hutt Valley in 1847-48. Before the wars were finished, fighting had ripped through Taranaki, the Waikato, the Bay of Plenty, Poverty Bay, the Urewera, parts of Hawke's Bay and the Central Plateau.

Historians don't all agree on what the wars meant. Some argue that Maori won. Some argue that the settlers won. But what most agree on is that these wars helped make New Zealand what it is today. It even gave us some of our roads and towns. The Great South Road, in Auckland, was built in the early 1860s by the British army so they could invade the King Country. Cambridge was a war town. Hamilton was named after a naval captain killed at Gate Pa in 1864.

Author collection/Heroes of Peace and War

WHO FOUGHT THE WARS?

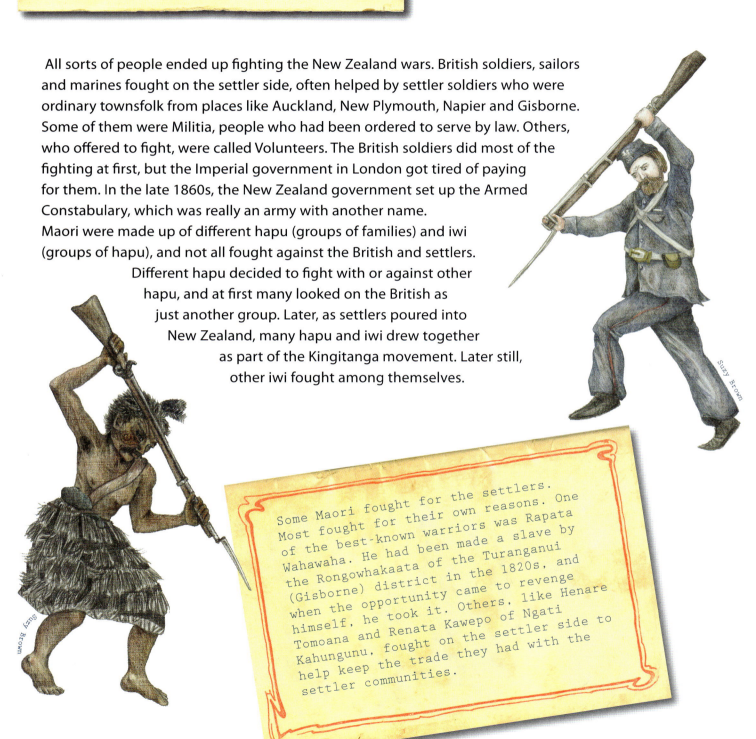

All sorts of people ended up fighting the New Zealand wars. British soldiers, sailors and marines fought on the settler side, often helped by settler soldiers who were ordinary townsfolk from places like Auckland, New Plymouth, Napier and Gisborne. Some of them were Militia, people who had been ordered to serve by law. Others, who offered to fight, were called Volunteers. The British soldiers did most of the fighting at first, but the Imperial government in London got tired of paying for them. In the late 1860s, the New Zealand government set up the Armed Constabulary, which was really an army with another name.

Maori were made up of different hapu (groups of families) and iwi (groups of hapu), and not all fought against the British and settlers. Different hapu decided to fight with or against other hapu, and at first many looked on the British as just another group. Later, as settlers poured into New Zealand, many hapu and iwi drew together as part of the Kingitanga movement. Later still, other iwi fought among themselves.

Some Maori fought for the settlers. Most fought for their own reasons. One of the best-known warriors was Rapata Wahawaha. He had been made a slave by the Rongowhakaata of the Turanganui (Gisborne) district in the 1820s, and when the opportunity came to revenge himself, he took it. Others, like Henare Tomoana and Renata Kawepo of Ngati Kahungunu, fought on the settler side to help keep the trade they had with the settler communities.

WHY THE WARS STARTED

The New Zealand Wars were fought for many reasons, but the main one was the fact that Britain was colonising New Zealand. While Maori liked the idea of trade, many saw their lands and culture disappearing because of settler farms, towns, roads, ports and industries.

The British thought colonisation was going to be good for Maori people. People in the Colonial Office — which ran the Empire for the British government — and the Church of England believed the British way was the best in the world, and the best way to help Maori was to educate them to live like the British. They stopped cannibalism. They stopped slavery. But they did much damage as well. Well-meaning missionaries did not realise that Maori were more comfortable living by their own customs.

By the 1830s Australian merchants were buying land in New Zealand. They did not obey any laws, and the local British Resident, James Busby, was a laughing stock because he had no power. Law was one of the most important things to the British, and the idea of a lawless New Zealand was terrible. Then, in 1839, a businessman named Edward Gibbon Wakefield announced that he was going to set up his own private colony in New Zealand.

The Colonial Office had to do something, but they had no money. They decided to set up a British administration in New Zealand, securing Maori help with a treaty. This was the Treaty of Waitangi, which Captain William Hobson organised in February 1840. It was written in a hurry, ineptly translated into Maori, and none of the British officials really knew whether 'sovereignty' meant the same thing to Maori as it did to them.

William Hobson (1792-1842), naval commander and first Governor of New Zealand.

Edward Gibbon Wakefield (1796-1862), social dreamer and founder of the New Zealand Company.

The Resident's house, Waitangi, has been preserved and restored. The Treaty of Waitangi was signed on the lawn in the foreground.

While the Colonial Office organised the Treaty, Edward Gibbon Wakefield's agents bought land from Maori between Taranaki and the north of the South Island. But they too were badly organised, and in some places bought land from Maori who did not have any rights to what they were selling.

It was a complete mess. Poor old Governors Hobson, Willoughby Shortland and Robert FitzRoy had their work cut out for them, trying to sort it all out without aggravating Maori on one hand and the Wakefield settlers on the other. Maori in Wellington, Wanganui and New Plymouth were particularly annoyed by the way they had been treated. By 1844, FitzRoy expected there would be war.

WAR IN THE NORTH   1845–46

The first of the New Zealand Wars was fought in the Bay of Islands between the British and some hapu from Nga Puhi on one side, led by Tamati Waka Nene, and hapu from Nga Puhi on the other, led by Hone Wiremu Heke Pokai (Hone Heke). Hone Heke was the first to sign the Treaty of Waitangi in 1840. He hoped the agreement would bring trade, people and prosperity, but was disappointed. Hobson moved the capital from Waitangi to Auckland, which took away a lot of the trade. He also raised duties on what was left. Heke thought the Treaty had given Maori the right to rule themselves. He didn't want to start a war, he just wanted the trade he thought Maori had been promised. He decided to protest by chopping down the flagpole above Kororareka (Russell). He talked about it a great deal around the Bay of Islands and nobody was surprised when he sent his right-hand-man, Te Haratua, to knock the flagpole over in July 1844.

FitzRoy was not happy, and by way of a lesson to all Maori decided to make an example of Heke. He asked for soldiers from Australia, rushed up to the Bay of Islands, and put the flagpole up. By this time Heke had a new ally, Te Ruki Kawiti, another Nga Puhi chief.

They agreed to talk and at first all seemed well, but Heke was still not happy and chopped the flagpole down a second time in January 1845. FitzRoy asked for more troops and had the flagpole put up again. The arrival of soldiers looked like war to a lot of the settlers. 'How will the Maoris like cold steel?' some of the Kororareka people foolishly declared. Heke was unafraid. 'I will cut down the flagstaff'.

He did, too, but he now had to deal with the soldiers guarding the pole, and that meant he had to fight. In March, Kawiti attacked Kororareka while Heke chopped down the pole. A ferocious battle surged back and forth around the town, and when the Kororareka gunpowder store blew up by accident the British decided to leave. Heke's men knew the battle was over, and even helped take the settlers to ships waiting in the Bay of Islands.

Heke hadn't intended things to go that far, and he now had a war on his hands. FitzRoy called for more help, and by April 1845 nearly 1000 men of the 58th Regiment were on their way to the Bay of Islands. They found an ally in Tamati Waka Nene, who also wanted trade with the British but decided that co-operating, not protesting, was the better way to get it.

Hone Wiremu Heke Pokai (c.1807–50), left, with Eruera Maihi Patuone (?–1872).

Te Ruki Kawiti (c.1770s–1854), known to settlers as 'The Duke'.

Heke built a pa (fort) on a narrow piece of land at Puketutu, between a forest and Lake Omapere. At the beginning of May a large force of British soldiers and Nene's men arrived outside Heke's pa. It was very strong and had been designed to stop musket balls, which Maori knew all about from their own wars a few years before. These pa were named 'musket pa'.

Colonel Hulme, the commander of the 58th Regiment, had no artillery, though he did have a few Congreve rockets. These were giant fireworks, all noise and very little bang. Heke's defences were not complete, and Hulme tried to get his soldiers around to the back of the pa, which was still open. The British soldiers who did get to the rear were ambushed by Kawiti's men. Although the British had to retreat, Heke abandoned the pa the next day. The next month the British tried again. Kawiti built a musket pa at Ohaeawai. The British were led by Colonel Henry Despard, who knew very little about New Zealand. He knew artillery was needed to knock down musket pa, but his first bombardment did not do much because he did not have heavy enough guns.

Battle for Ohaeawai. A sketch by Sergeant John Williams, 58th Regiment.

One of the big 32-pounders finally arrived from HMS *Hazard*. This started battering down the walls of the pa, and Kawiti's men rushed out to try and stop it. Despard decided to send his soldiers against the walls. This was silly before the walls had been broken, and Nene tried to stop him, but nobody was supposed to tell colonels what to do. In the end Nene said something rude in Maori. 'What did he say?' Despard demanded. 'The chief says you are a very stupid person', his translator explained. This was not the thing to say to a colonel, and the very stupid person stubbornly went ahead with his attack. Of course it failed.

British troops attack Heke's pa near Puketutu.

> **IT'S A FACT**
>
> The British did not copy trench warfare from Maori and then use it in the First World War. This was suggested in the 1980s and has been repeated since as if true, but in fact both peoples invented it themselves, at different times.

Rifle pits can still be seen at Ruapekapeka pa.

More big guns finally arrived. Kawiti knew his defences couldn't handle that sort of blasting for long, and slipped away with his men under cover of darkness.

Meanwhile, New Zealand got a new governor. FitzRoy was replaced by George Grey. By the time Grey arrived, FitzRoy was already halfway to sorting out peace with Heke and Kawiti, but Grey wanted to teach them a lesson.

Kawiti was in a new pa by this time — Ruapekapeka, the Bat's Lair. It was a very strong place, in the hills behind the Bay of Islands. Kawiti knew that if this was lost, Nene would consider the war over. And the war was as much between Nga Puhi as it was between Nga Puhi and British. Grey's troops spent days dragging big guns up to the pa. Soon after New Year 1846, they opened fire with a storm of shells. Kawiti's men tried to fire back, but had to abandon the pa.

A few weeks later Kawiti and Heke surrendered. They could not fight any longer. Nene and the British had won. Grey wanted to strip Kawiti and Heke of their lands, but eventually gave them a generous peace settlement. Kawiti knew he had been beaten by artillery. 'Had they nothing but muskets,' the old chief grumbled later, 'I should be in my pa at the present time.'

> **IT'S A FACT**
>
> Artillery in the nineteenth and even the twentieth century was often named after the weight of shell it fired. Other guns and weapons were named after their inventors. The British used 24-pounders, 32-pounders, Cohorn mortars, and Congreve and Armstrong rockets during the wars.

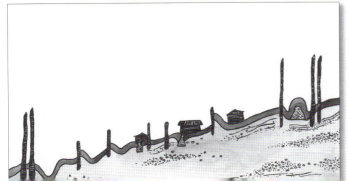

A side view of Ruapekapeka pa.

THE WELLINGTON WAR
1846–47

The war in the north was hardly over when more trouble blew up in Wellington and the Hutt Valley. Maori were upset at the way their land had been 'bought' by Wakefield's New Zealand Company. The same land was also under control of Ngati Toa chiefs Te Rauparaha and Te Rangihaeata. What it boiled down to was that the New Zealand Company claimed the Hutt Valley. So did Ngati Tama and Ngati Rangitahi, two hapu under Te Rauparaha's rule.

In February 1847 Governor Grey sent Lieutenant-Colonel Hulme and nearly 350 soldiers to occupy a farm in the middle of the Hutt Valley belonging to the settler Boulcott. There were several small battles. Finally, one foggy morning in May, a taua (war party) of 200 Maori toa (warriors) under upper Whanganui chief Hemi Topine te Mamaku crawled up the banks of the Hutt River and attacked 45 men of the 58th Regiment.

Te Mamaku underestimated the power of the regiment. The British were very good at fighting in the open, and drove the taua back over the Hutt River.

Samuel Brees (1810–65) drew this picture of the Hutt River, near Molesworth's Farm, in 1846.

Boulcott's stockade after the Battle of Boulcott's Farm. The picket fence in the foreground surrounds soldiers' graves.

12

George Hyde Page. Alexander Turnbull Library. G-525

The fight at Battle Hill, August 1846.

Grey then decided to attack Te Rangihaeata, who lived in a pa at Pauahatanui. When news came of Maori reinforcements arriving from Wanganui, Grey decided to arrest Te Rauparaha. That didn't stop Te Rangihaeata. When Grey finally attacked Te Rangihaeata's pa, Matai-taua, at the head of the Pauahatanui inlet, he found the chief had left and was on his way north.

The British set off in pursuit, with the help of toa from Te Atiawa. They pushed ahead through dense and damp forests, and finally caught up with Te Rangihaeata and his men atop a steep hill, halfway to Paekakariki. They couldn't take the hilltop and left Te Atiawa to lay siege to it. A few days later Te Rangihaeata escaped, fleeing to the Horowhenua where he built another pa at Poroutawhao.

The war turned to Wanganui, then known as Petrie, where another of the Wakefield land deals had gone wrong. In May, farmer J.A. Gillfillian and his family were attacked by a group of Maori. The supposed murderers were found and hanged, and soon afterwards Te Mamaku took a very powerful taua south to attack Petrie.

They besieged the town, but unlike the British, Maori could not both fight and feed themselves, and the men were needed for the planting season. Te Mamaku tried to win the war quickly, but neither side won the battle that followed at St John's Wood. Te Mamaku withdrew under a white flag, and Grey sent his favourite negotiator, Donald McLean, to sort out the problem.

IT'S A FACT

When Te Rauparaha was arrested he was taken back to Wellington in the paddle steamer *Driver*. During the journey clouds of steam poured into Te Rauparaha's cabin. He thought it was the British trying to kill him, but actually it was because the *Driver* had very old and leaky boilers.

WHERE'S BOULCOTT'S FARM TODAY?

You can find a monument to the Battle of Boulcott's Farm in the middle of Lower Hutt. It's on the corner of High Street and Military Road. The battle was fought on what is now the golf course, near the river.

WHERE'S THE SITE OF TE RANGIHAEATA'S LAST BATTLE TODAY?

The hill Te Rangihaeata climbed at the end of the Wellington war is near the Paekakariki Hill Road, between Pauatahanui and Paekakariki. Look for the signs labelled 'Battle Hill', drive in, and obey the signs. Be ready for a long, hard climb to get there. Te Rangihaeata's trenches are still visible at the top as a faint zig-zag.

Battle Hill is a hard climb, even without people shooting at you from above.

St Alban's Church and a graveyard were established on top of Matai-taua pa and the British redoubt at the head of the Pauahatanui inlet. This view, across one of the gravestones, looks down on the inlet.

THE TARANAKI WAR

The war that broke out in Taranaki in 1860 has often been called a land war. It was fought over the sale of the Waitara Block, a piece of land north of New Plymouth that had the best harbour in the region.

An artist's impression of New Plymouth, early 1840s.

However, the war was also about sovereignty, the right to rule. The British thought Maori had signed away their sovereignty in the Treaty of Waitangi, but the Maori version of the Treaty did not say this. Chiefs wanted to carry on the way they always had, and didn't like what they saw as British interference. At the same time, settlers and goods such as blankets, muskets, tobacco and other things were changing the way Maori lived. It was a frightening time, and by the 1850s many Maori thought something should be done about it.
This led to the Kingitanga movement, organised by a Ngati Haua chief, Te Waharoa Tarapipipi, who the British called Wiremu Tamihana (William Thompson). Te Waharoa and others managed to persuade many hapu and iwi to make Te Wherowhero of the Waikato iwi their king. That became a separate sovereignty in the middle of the North Island. Their war leader was Rewi Maniapoto, one of the greatest commanders of his time.

All this was very important for Taranaki. The land had been bought by the New Zealand Company in 1839–40, but it was also claimed by Waikato iwi who had conquered it during the musket wars. This meant that the Kingitanga movement joined the argument over the Waitara Block, and this is partly why the Taranaki war was also a war of sovereignty.

Te Waharoa Tarapipipi (18??–66), of Ngati Haua, adopted the Christian names Wiremu Tamihana (William Thompson) when he was baptised in 1839.

15

THE WAR FOR WAITARA, MARCH 1860–MARCH 1861

The Waitara Block was owned by Te Atiawa, whose chief, Te Rangitake, was known to the British as Wiremu Kingi (William King). He did not stand for nonsense from the British. By March 1860 it looked like both sides were going to fight over the block. British forces included sailors from the steamship HMS *Niger*, under Captain Peter Cracroft, and much of the 65th Regiment of Foot, under Colonel E.C. Gold. They were joined by Volunteers and Militia from New Plymouth.

Te Rangitake's war leader was a fiery warrior named Hapurona, a talented commander. At first they did not have many men, but Te Rangitake hoped to get support from the King Country. In March 1860 he built a pa at Te Kohia, on the edge of the Waitara Block, to show he had claim to it. This was nicknamed the 'L-pa' because of its shape. One historian has said that Te Rangitake and Hapurona built the L-pa quickly so they could abandon it without losing anything. In fact, we know they expected to stay in the L-pa because they moved huge stores of food into it. It had to be built quickly so that the British would not get time to attack it half-finished. As it was, the British set out to attack it the day after it was completed.

Te Rangitake, Wiremu Kingi (William King) (c.1795–1882).

Hapurona, fighting chief of Te Atiawa.

The British camp at Waitara. A watercolour by Charles Emilius Gold (1809–71).

The British had a fearsome number of big guns, rockets, sailors and soldiers. They knew how to bash down walls with guns, and by late afternoon on 17 March had knocked a hole in the palisades. By this time it was getting dark, so Colonel Gold decided to wait until the next morning to attack, but Te Rangitake escaped overnight. Like Kawiti, they had been blown out of the pa by artillery, and there was no point losing lives for nothing. Gold decided to attack Ngati Ruanui, who were raiding settler houses south of New Plymouth. That campaign ended when sailors from the *Niger* captured Kaipopo pa. But it wasn't much of a victory. Captain Cracroft declared they had struggled against 'about a hundred' Maori. In fact the pa was virtually empty, and the sailors leap-frogged into it, jumping up and over each other's backs to climb the wall.

In June, a powerful taua arrived from the King Country, joining Te Rangitake's forces at a new pa, Puketakauere. The British attacked, but the battle ended when a force of sailors tried to rush into the pa and were shot down. The British went back to Camp Waitara to lick their wounds. 'Thank God my life was spared', one soldier wrote in his diary. This sort of defeat was very embarrassing, and the British sent Major-General Thomas Pratt to take over. He was a tall, thin man, very old but very experienced, and he had his own ideas about fighting. By this time Te Rangitake had been joined by another party from the King Country, under Te Wetini Taiporutu of Ngati Haua. Te Wetini challenged the British to fight him atop Mahoetahi Hill, hoping to ambush them with Te Rangitake's help.

Mahoetahi Hill today.

'The approaches to Te Arei', a page from the notebook of Henry Warre.

Te Rangitake didn't like this idea, and rightly so. Pratt set up a trap of his own, sending men from both New Plymouth and Waitara to ambush Te Wetini's force. In the battle that followed, Te Wetini's forces were destroyed.

At the end of 1860 the war turned to the hills behind New Plymouth, where Te Atiawa lived. The way was barred by a long climb up to two pa known as Te Arei and Pukerangiora. If they could be taken, the war would be over. Hapurona decided to defend it with a 'chain fortress', a string of small pa. Each had to be taken before the next could be attacked.

Pratt decided to destroy the chain by digging trenches, or saps, backed by forts of his own. Saps were a very old method for attacking forts that the British had been using for hundreds of years. But saps were also very slow to dig, very expensive, and not very heroic. 'Sappy Pratt' was criticised by the settlers and the government for making his men dig instead of charging at the enemy. But the strategy worked.

Hapurona knew his own defences were in danger. In January 1861 he tried to attack the British redoubt near his main pa of Huirangi. They did their best, but when Hapurona saw the British trench diggers hacking their way towards Huirangi, he knew it was time to go.

The British dug on, and by February they were halfway up the slopes to Pukerangiora. Hapurona did everything he could to stop them, but the sweating trench diggers pushed on, week after week. It was obvious that Pukerangiora would fall, and on 19 March a white flag went up over the pa. Te Rangitake left for Kikihiki, and Hapurona took over peace negotiations.

Governor Thomas Robert Gore-Browne was very pleased the war had ended, and made arrangements for the titles to land in Waitara to be investigated. But he was also worried about the way the Kingitanga movement had been involved, and thought Waikato should be attacked.

A modern-day view from Te Arei down the Waitotara River. British forces advanced up the ridge on the left in 1860–61.

A surviving stretch of the sap dug by British soldiers during the approach to Pukerangiora. The ridges along it are traverses, zig-zags designed to stop anybody being able to shoot straight down the trench.

WHAT BATTLES WERE LIKE

The battles of the New Zealand wars were nasty. There was usually only time for musketeers to fire one or two shots before they had to fight their opponent hand to hand using bayonets, patu, fists, kicking, strangling or even head-butting. Soldiers were sometimes sent against palisades with nothing more than swords. Battles were noisy, dirty, messy, very violent and very, very dangerous.

Even in the 1860s, when Enfield rifles fired faster and further, battles could only be won if the men got to grips with each other. Cannon blew people apart or riddled them with what was known as 'grape shot', a whole cannon-load of small bullets. Grown men screamed, howled and wept during the fighting. It was simply awful.

Afterwards, the wounded were usually taken back to medical tents or pa, but this was before the days of antibiotics. Neither Maori tohunga nor settler doctors could do much other than let nature take its course.

WHERE ARE THE TARANAKI PA TODAY?

Many Taranaki war sites can be reached from New Plymouth. Mahoetahi is a hill on Devon Road, about 4 km from Waitara. To get to Pratt's Sap, turn right up the Waitara Road and go past all the redoubts, which are signposted. At the top is a reserve, with what's left of Te Arei pa and the remains of the trenches dug with so much effort around 150 years ago.

Maori fire into British positions. This sketch is by Lieutenant H.S. Bates of the 65th Regiment.

19

THE WAIKATO WAR

The Waikato war was about sovereignty, and it was started by George Grey, who came back to New Zealand as Governor in 1861. He spent nearly two years telling the British government how dangerous New Zealand had become. This was not true, but the British couldn't really tell from the other side of the world, and when other reports from New Zealand seemed to agree with Grey, they began sending more regiments.

Of course Grey couldn't just start a war. He had to pretend that Maori had started it. He did this in two ways. First, he told everybody that Rewi was planning to attack Auckland. This was an excuse to start building a road from Auckland down to the Waikato River. Then, in early 1863, Grey managed to upset Maori in Taranaki to the point where a new war started there.

The war in Taranaki meant the Kingitanga movement was involved — and Grey suddenly had his reason to attack the King Country. It was sneaky, and all down to politics.

Lieutenant-General Sir Duncan Alexander Cameron (1808-88) seen here in later life.

George Grey (1812-98), twice Governor of New Zealand, and the man who started the Waikato war.

LIEUTENANT-GENERAL CAMERON

British forces in the Waikato war were led by Lieutenant-General Cameron, a very experienced soldier who had fought in the Crimean War. He was a good deal cleverer than some historians have tried to tell us, and was definitely a match for Rewi. Of course he also had four times the number of men Rewi had, all the boats, lots of heavy guns, and more supplies. Even a foolish general could have won the Waikato war with all that. But Cameron was not foolish, and even though he had every possible advantage, he still worked out clever ways of fighting, because he didn't want too many of his men killed.

IT'S A FACT

One day during the Waikato campaign, Lieutenant-General Cameron invited a captured Maori chief to dinner, explaining that he didn't have any potatoes. Then he released the chief. A while later several canoes came upriver loaded with potatoes — a present from the enemy.

THE WAR DOWN THE WAIKATO RIVER, JULY 1863–JANUARY 1864

Rewi Maniapoto knew he had a problem when General Cameron's regiments moved into the King Country in July 1863. The British had riverboats that could steam past Maori defences down the river, all the way to the capital at Ngaruawahia. Cameron did not want to fight a winter campaign. He advanced only as far as the ridges of the Mangatawhiri River, near Mercer. Here the 12th and 14th regiments were attacked by 400 toa under Te Huirama of Ngati Mahuta. In the middle of the battle Cameron led the charge, pushing Te Huirama's forces back to the Maramarua.

Cameron was recommended for the Victoria Cross, but he didn't get one. Lieutenant-Generals were not supposed to lead heroic charges.

Then he sat down to build up his supplies and wait for his gunboats to arrive. Everything he needed came down the Great South Road, and Ngati Paoa, allied to Maniapoto, began attacking the supply convoys. The British began sending special bush rangers into the hills, some of them led by the Austrian adventurer Gustavus von Tempsky.

Williamson's Clearing, Great South Road, 1863.

Spring came. Rewi Maniapoto knew Cameron was going to attack down the Waikato River, so he put much of his force into Meremere, with some captured cannons. Unfortunately they did not have proper ammunition.

The result was that when Cameron steamed up in the brand new paddle-wheel gunboat *Pioneer*, Maori could do nothing. They blazed away with muskets and the old cannon, but the *Pioneer* sat there with Cameron and newspaper reporters on board while the bullets clanged off her iron armour.

Rewi Manga Maniapoto (1815–94).

HMS *Pioneer* at anchor in the Waikato, engaging Maori batteries at Meremere.

When Cameron used his gunboats to tow barges filled with troops up the river, past Meremere, Rewi pulled back to Rangiriri. The British were delighted with their easy victory. 'It really is very exciting now', one soldier wrote.

Rewi had no intention of giving up, but he needed to fight where he had some chance of winning. Rangiriri looked to be the place. A wall, redoubt and trench were built across the road, between the Waikato River and Lake Waikare.

In mid-November, Cameron made plans to cut behind Maori defences with his gunboats. However, the boats ran aground on the way upstream and then tangled in shallow water near the pa. While they organised themselves, Cameron decided to attack the defences with his regiments, which were lined up at the front.

Rewi's forces shot down the attackers as they came. Some of the trenches were taken, but the main redoubt held firm. Many men were left standing in a deep ditch ahead of the main wall. William Mair, an interpreter, called this the 'greatest blunder of the day'. There was a gap in the wall, from behind which a lot of Maori were firing guns. Whenever anybody passed the gap — which they had to in order to attack — a 'fearful hailstorm of bullets whortled through'.

By this time some of the men had come ashore from the boats. They managed to push some defenders towards the Waikare Swamp, but the redoubt held firm. As dark fell, Cameron sent sailors to take the redoubt, but they were met with a 'deadly volley.' Colonel Mould suggested digging a sap. Cameron agreed.

Next morning, to everyone's surprise, a white flag flew over the redoubt. The story went that the defenders had run out of bullets and wanted a truce so they could ask for more. In fact, most of the defenders had pulled out. Rewi decided that he couldn't fight Cameron's numbers, and wanted to preserve his army.

It was a clever tactic, and although Cameron now had Rangiriri, he still hadn't defeated Rewi's army. Nor could he advance, as he was waiting on more stores from Auckland. By the beginning of December he was ready to start again, and he took his boats and men upriver to the Kingitanga movement's capital, Ngaruawahia, which had been abandoned. Once again, Rewi foiled Cameron's efforts to fight a decisive battle.

Supply barges under tow outside Ngaruawahia, early 1864.

A BRITISH HERO

This is a nineteenth century view of Lieutenant Colonel McNeill's rescue of Private Vosper during the battle of the Mangapiko River on 11 February 1864. It shows us what the artist wanted people to see; a great British hero knocking over Maori. That's different from what actually happened. We have to be careful when we look at pictures and stories that show history, because sometimes they don't tell us exactly what went on.

HEROES AND MEDALS

A lot of soldiers won medals such as the New Zealand Cross during the New Zealand Wars. Others won the Victoria Cross, which Queen Victoria set up a few years previous to the New Zealand Cross. At the time, The Victoria Cross was the very highest military medal. The problem was that these medals were so new that nobody really knew what you had to do in order to win them. New Zealand explorer Charles Heaphy got his by asking for it — and after a while it arrived.

A nineteenth-century view of Lieutenant-Colonel McNeill's rescue of Private Vosper during the battle of the Mangapiko River, 11 February 1864.

Matthew Wright

WHERE'S RANGIRIRI TODAY?

The Rangiriri fortification is easy to get to; it's right on State Highway 1, near Rangiriri itself. You can still see part of the trenches, which have been fenced and preserved. The graveyard where those who fell is nearby, and there's a private museum across the road.

> **IT'S A FACT**
> The *Pioneer* had two 12-pounder guns in rotating iron gun-houses. One of these metal cylinders was later taken ashore at Meremere and used as the police lock-up.

Wilson and Horton, Alexander Turnbull Library, C-033-004

This is how one artist thought things looked when Hauraki Tonganui answered William Mair's peace offer.

THE LEGEND OF REWI'S LAST STAND, MARCH 1864

By early 1864, Rewi had decided to defend the Waipa and Punui rivers, southwest of Ngaruawahia. To do this he built New Zealand's biggest fort, a huge set of trenches and redoubts between Paterangi and Pikopiko. It was tremendously strong, and by January 1864 he had 2000 toa to defend it. Cameron had only about 2100 men, and knew he couldn't attack. In February he sent just

Soldiers making gabions, Pukerimu, early 1864, possibly for service at Orakau.

over 1000 men around the side of the defences to Te Awamutu instead.

The Waikato alliance broke up. Tamihana pulled his own people back to Maungatautari, hoping to stop the British there, while Rewi took Ngati Maniapoto to Puniu. They still wanted to fight, and in March Rewi was persuaded by a group of Ngati Raukawa and Urewera to join them near Orakau. The idea was that they could force the British into a fight and beat them. Rewi wasn't sure, but went along with it.

The pa lacked water, and wasn't finished before Brigadier-General George Carey attacked. William Mair ended up lying under a cart 'about 400 yards from their pa, and all night long the bullets were screaming past and over us.' Finally the British began digging another trench. Cameron arrived to see what was happening, and on the third day sent Mair to ask the Maori to surrender.

Mair ended up talking to Hauraki Tonganui of Taupo, but the words were always said to be Rewi's, and went something like: 'Friend, I shall fight against you for ever, for ever!' Nobody knows precisely what was said because several versions were written down. But the general idea is the same.

Then something extraordinary happened. The firing died away, and the British saw the defenders emerge from the south side of the pa. Rewi had ordered them to break out despite the odds. The men were protecting the women and children, who were in the middle of the group, and they quickly moved for the bush.

The British gave chase, but could not catch them even though von Tempsky's Forest Rangers 'bounded over the ground as if their feet had wings …'

THE BATTLE OF GATE PA — March 1864

By early 1864 there was trouble around Tauranga, where Ngai te Rangi had been friendly to the Kingitanga movement. In the end, their chief, Rawiri Tuaia, challenged the British to a fight. The local commander, Colonel Greer, decided not to, so Rawiri built a pa for him to attack. Greer refused, and Rawiri built another pa, much closer to Tauranga, right across the main south road at a place known as Pukehinahina. The British called it Gate Pa, after the gate in the road.

Governor Grey sent Cameron and reinforcements from Auckland by ship. All sorts of guns came ashore, including a gigantic 110-pounder Armstrong, the biggest gun in New Zealand.

Cameron put part of the 68th Regiment behind Gate Pa to stop the defenders getting away. Then he lined up the rest of his men and all the guns, and at the end of March opened fire on the trenches. As one soldier remarked:

> An awful fire was concentrated on our redoubt… shells were bursting all round. Our fences and frail parapets crumbled away under the heavy artillery fire, and splinters and earth were continually flying through the air. We were every now and then smothered with the dirt thrown up by the exploding shells … soon converted into mud.

British artillery at Gate Pa, just after sunrise, 29 April 1864. Lieutenant-General Sir Duncan Cameron stands with forage cap and shooting stick against the carriage wheel.

Photographer unknown, Alexander Turnbull Library, F-29252-1/2

26

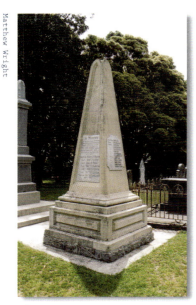

Maori defences at Gate Pa extended down this hill, beside what is now Cameron Road.

This monument to some of the fallen soldiers is in the historic cemetery near Tauranga's town centre.

Despite all the noise and smoke, they didn't do a lot of damage. This was because the biggest guns didn't drop shells into the pa. They went whizzing along at ground level. A lot of shells bounced on the soft ground and didn't hit the target.
Around 4 o'clock, Cameron sent the troops into a gap on the left side of the pa. They pushed some of the defenders out, but others had been safe inside deep rifle pits and the storming party were surprised. A battle broke out in the narrow trenches. At that moment Captain Hamilton of HMS *Esk* arrived with his bluejackets — and was shot dead as he led an attack. As dusk fell, the battered British poured out of the pa, leaving their dead and wounded behind.
But once again, Maori could not hold it. Some gave water to the wounded British during the night, and then slipped away.

WHERE'S GATE PA?

Gate Pa (Pukehinahina) is inside Tauranga. You can find the Monmouth Redoubt beside the police station near the waterfront. Head south down Cameron Road. About 3 km south of the town centre you'll see the Gate Pa RSA Bowling Club, which is built over some of the trenches. On the left, St George's Memorial Chapel stands in a small park, where the redoubt used to be. They didn't build the road through a historic site — the road was there first.

A REALLY DANGEROUS FACT

The shells that bounced past Gate Pa ended up buried kilometres beyond. People were digging them up for years, and some were even found in the 1980s. They didn't blow up, but they could have...

Gate Pa

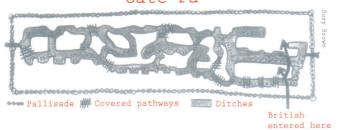

27

FOOD, HORRIBLE FOOD

There was one problem with the food served up to the British soldiers during the New Zealand Wars. It was horrible. After a couple of weeks on the march all the good stuff had usually been eaten and rations got boring — and nasty. During the Ohaeawai campaign in 1845 the men ran out of everything except flour and scraps of mutton, so they ate it boiled in their billies. They called it 'skillie', which probably helped disguise the fact that just about the same recipe was also used to make wallpaper paste, only without the mutton. Midshipman H. McKillop, a British sailor who fought during the northern war of 1845 and the Wellington war of 1846–47, remembered the way hungry sailors made do one cold night after the battle of Horokiwi in August 1846.

> " There were many extraordinary modes of cooking invented this night — such as frying pork in a tin drinking-cup, grilling pigeons on ramrods, boiling water in a glass bottle, and such like. Hunger being the best sauce, enabled us to make a hearty meal; and we soon forgot our little privations, and should have been jolly enough, had not the loss of poor Blackburn ... cast a gloom over our little party. "

During the Taranaki war, Grace Hirst sent 'tea, coffee, butter, sugar, meat, pies, pouffs, etc' to her husband at Huia Fort, which wasn't far away. Other men were stationed near hotels and could buy hot meals. Quite often the men ended up raiding a local farmhouse for food. Settlers liked the idea of soldiers coming through to protect them, but sometimes it was like having a plague of locusts drop in to visit. Everything got eaten.

General Cameron knew food was a problem, which was why his Waikato campaign was so slow. He often had to wait for enough supplies to be delivered. Even then, the men thought it was dull — 'sour bread, no butter, boiled beef every day, Sunday boiled pork, coffee and tea, sugar, buy our own milk.' But they did not go hungry, which was better than Colonel Whitmore managed in 1868 when he was chasing Te Kooti. His men ran out of food in the Ruakituri River valley and had to eat some of their horses.

Regulars at mealtime. Tin mugs of soup were common fare in the wars. Robert Hustwick recalled that '... we all sit down on the ground with our grub on our legs ... I put my plate on my knees and a small tin of soup on boots.'

A DIFFERENT WAR 1864–66

After the battle of Orakau the Kingitanga movement did not want to fight any more. The government didn't either. Grey wanted to take land from Maori as punishment for what he saw as rebellion. The settler government wanted to take even more. The new Premier, Frederick Weld, had the idea of 'self sufficiency', meaning New Zealand would look after its own defences. The Imperial troops began to leave.

But the wars were far from over. Taranaki had never calmed down after the wars of 1860–61 and 1863, and by 1864 there was more trouble. A new religion emerged, called Pai Marire by its founder, Te Ua Haumene. He taught that the colonists would be driven away without fighting but with the help of angels. But not all his followers agreed. Some wanted to take up the fight. They regarded Pai Marire as a way to draw Maori together.

The settlers were very frightened, especially when a Pai Marire war party attacked British soldiers at Te Ahuahu in 1864, killed them, and took their heads. By the end of the year there was talk of a Pai Marire attack on Wanganui, led by Matene te Rangitauia. But when the Pai Marire attacked British forces at Sentry Hill they were totally defeated.

Hori Kingi te Anaua, John White (1826–91) and Te Ua Haumene (?–1866), around 1860.

Pai Marire ceremony at Taratoa, 27 January 1865.

Herbert Meade, Alexander Turnbull Library, B-139-014

PUTTING HEADS TOGETHER

The Pai Marire wars had a lot to do with heads, and not ones attached to their owners. The most famous was the head of Captain T.W.J. Lloyd of the 57th Regiment. He was killed by Pai Marire at the battle of Te Ahuahu in April 1864, and his head was taken away for preserving.

The British wanted Lloyd's head back. When the interpreter Charles Broughton found out it was at Pehiatu pa near Waitotara, he decided to ride into the pa by himself and ask for it. To his surprise, Pai Marire leader Te Ua Haumene handed the head over.

There was more head trouble a few years later, when the government offered to pay for the heads of any of Te Kooti or Titokowaru's men. Of course they didn't actually want the heads, it was just a way of saying they were offering money for getting rid of their enemy. But both Colonel Whitmore and J.C. Richardson ended up with sackloads of these trophies.

There was a reason for this. When Te Keepa's men started taking the heads of dead Pai Marire after one battle in 1868, the settler commander tried to stop them. Te Keepa took them anyway. 'If we can't prove we killed them,' he apparently explained, 'we won't be paid.'

WAR ON THE EAST COAST 1865–66

While things went from bad to worse in south Taranaki, some Pai Marire went to the Bay of Plenty. One group, led by Kereropa te Rau, ended up in Opotiki, where they murdered the local priest Carl Sylvius Volkner. This terrified the settlers, and was intended to draw other Maori to the Pai Marire cause.

A war followed around the East Cape. Te Arawa sided with the government, but some Urewera and others sided with the Pai Marire. Settler officers such as the brothers William and Gilbert Mair led some of these allied Maori war parties, but others were led by Maori themselves. The government's biggest ally was Rapata Wahawaha.

The East Coast war ended with a siege at Waerenga-a-hika, a pa just outside Turanganui (Gisborne). Here Pai Marire fought for a week before surrendering. The survivors were taken prisoner and sent to the Chatham Islands.

Donald McLean (1820–77), one of the most powerful men in New Zealand during the late 1860s.

IT'S A FACT

Rapata Wahawaha was known as 'Major Ropata' to the settlers. This was because of the way Donald McLean, who was a Scot, pronounced Rapata — and it stuck. 'Major Ropata' liked his new name — Rapata was the name given to him when he was a slave in the 1820s; he preferred not to be reminded of his misfortune.

The Tutaekuri River, with Omarunui beyond. Settler forces and kupapa assembled in the foreground, crossed the river, and attacked in what some called a massacre.

THE BATTLE OF OMARUNUI, OCTOBER 1866

After Pai Marire missionaries had come through the East Coast they went south to Hawke's Bay. This district had been peaceful for years, and neither settlers nor local Maori, Ngati Kahungunu, really wanted the newcomers. However, Ngati Hineuru at Te Haroto adopted Pai Marire teachings. They had been arguing with Ngati Kahungunu for years over the government land purchases in Ahuriri, and this was what started the war of 1866.

Some people have called the Hawke's Bay's war a 'one-day war', because all the battles happened on the same day. In fact the war really started months earlier, when Pai Marire arrived at Te Haroto. Ngati Kahungunu chiefs wanted to attack them then, but Donald McLean, who was the Provincial Superintendent, thought they should talk instead. In October, a group of Pai Marire came down the road from Te Haroto towards Napier. Nobody knew why. There was talk of an attack on Napier, but in the end the newcomers sat in the nearby kainga of Omarunui. McLean tried to talk to them, but they would not listen, so he ordered the Militia commander George Whitmore to attack, while other Militia tackled another Pai Marire group near Petane (Bay View), north of Napier.

McLean and Whitmore couldn't stand each other, but that didn't stop them fighting the Pai Marire. The two battles that followed were won by the settlers. At Omarunui, the settlers ran across the Tutaekuri River and shot the Pai Marire out of the village. It was such a quick victory that there were claims that it had been a massacre, and some historians still say that today. But the record shows that McLean gave Pai Marire several chances to give up, and they replied that they intended to fight.

Omarunui village, looking back across the Tutaekuri River towards Redclyffe. This scene is after the battle of 12 October 1866.

WHERE'S OMARUNUI?

There is a monument to the battle on Omarunui Road. Go through Waiohiki on the southwest side of Taradale, turn right into Omarunui Road, head upstream about 2 km, and the monument is on the left in a vineyard. The actual battle site is a little further along.

This monument to the battle of Omarunui was built for the fiftieth anniversary in 1916.

TITOKOWARU'S WAR
June 1868–April 1869

The next war broke out in south Taranaki in 1868. The land of Ngati Ruahine chief Titokowaru was being confiscated and by mid-1868 he could take no more. He began issuing challenges to his neighbouring hapu and to the settlers. 'I shall not die,' he declared in his most famous letter. He also announced that he had begun to eat people. 'My throat is always open for the eating of human flesh.' It sounded very bloodthirsty, which was what Titokowaru wanted. He did not actually eat people himself because this interfered with his mana tapu (sacredness). But some of his men did dine on settlers. They even hacked up one soldier and took away part of his body. 'We have only got his legs,' William Hunter wrote to the local magistrate. 'I have written to the Government and to McDonnell; we must have some spare arms.' He meant guns, and probably didn't realise he was being funny.

Soon there was talk of war. Settler forces in the area were led by New Zealand-born Lieutenant-Colonel Thomas McDonnell, 'Fighting Mac' to his men. Titokowaru had only 70 men. He couldn't fight the government without the support of his neighbours, so he decided to show them what he could do by attacking a small government redoubt at Turuturumokai.

In August, the government sent McDonnell into the dense rata forests of south Taranaki to attack Titokowaru in his kainga, Te Ngutu o te Manu (The Beak of the Bird). There were too many settlers for Titokowaru to tackle, so he abandoned the kainga, leaving the settlers to burn some of the whare. A month later McDonnell tried to attack Titokowaru's neighbouring kainga of Ruaruru. This didn't go so well. The settler force got lost in the bush and blundered into the back of Te Ngutu o te Manu. McDonnell lost track of where everybody was, and was ambushed by Titokowaru's men. He decided to withdraw, but forgot to tell von Tempsky's soldiers, who waited for an order to attack, which never came. And then von Tempsky was shot dead.

McDonnell was in disgrace, Titokowaru got the support he wanted from his neighbours, and the settlers panicked. To make matters worse, another leader, Te Kooti, was fighting around Gisborne. Suddenly it looked as if the government forces were in trouble. In fact they were not, but Titokowaru had managed to frighten the people so

Lieutenant-Colonel Thomas McDonnell (1832–99).

thoroughly that the settler defeat at Te Ngutu o te Manu seemed bigger than it was. There was even an effort to change the government.

Defence Minister Theodore Haultain sent Colonel Whitmore to take over from McDonnell. Whitmore was a better commander than McDonnell, though not as popular owing to his temper. Whitmore tried to attack Titokowaru at Moturoa in November 1868. That attack failed, and the settlers were chased all the way back to Wairoa (Waverley).

To top it all off, Te Kooti launched a raid on the East Coast. Haultain ordered Whitmore to take the Armed Constabulary to Turanganui (Gisborne). The Colonel only did so after making sure there were enough men left to protect Patea.

One historian has argued that, at the time, Titokowaru threatened government control from New Plymouth to Wellington. However, the settlers were not short of soldiers. Titokowaru never did attack. He knew he was outnumbered, and was too sensible to try fighting them all.

The last round of Titokowaru's war came in February 1869. Titokowaru built a gigantic fortress near Nukumaru, known as Tauranga-ika. Whitmore thought it 'exceedingly strong', and made careful plans to attack it with artillery.

However, at the last minute Titokowaru abandoned the pa and took off into the bush with his people. Nobody really knows why. Whitmore gave chase, there was a brief battle at Otautu, and the war became a messy campaign in the bush. Titokowaru was hunted by Te Keepa and the settler forces. In April he ordered his last men to scatter and took refuge with Te Atiawa.

Gustavus Ferdinand von Tempsky (1828–68), in Armed Constabulary uniform in 1868. Von Tempsky was an Austrian mercenary, goldminer, adventurer and artist.

Hartley Webster, Webster Collection, Alexander Turnbull Library, PA2-2102

Suzy Brown

Lieutenant-Colonel
George S. Whitmore
(1830-1903).

LIEUTENANT-COLONEL SIR GEORGE STODDARD WHITMORE

Lieutenant-Colonel Whitmore was born in Malta. He fought with the British Army in the Crimea before arriving in New Zealand to take up the post of Military Secretary to Lieutenant-General Cameron.

In 1863 Whitmore left the army to settle in New Zealand, buying land in Hawke's Bay, a property he called Rissington after a village near where he had been brought up. The government appointed him a senior officer in the colonial forces.

He was a very tough man, able to out-walk just about anybody through the bush. But he was also a very short man, and he had a very short temper. All sorts of stories revolve around Whitmore's nasty moods. When he found out that the hill behind his Rissington house had been named after his station manager 'I demand a mountain named after me as well,' he declared. So his farmhands made one out of stable manure for him.

However, Whitmore was a very good soldier, and when he fought he often led the charge himself. Sometimes that didn't work. He was in front at Moturoa until he fell over his own coat-tails.

After the New Zealand Wars he became the commander of all New Zealand's defence forces, eventually retiring to Napier, where he died in 1903.

TE KOOTI'S ESCAPE 1865–66

Te Kooti Arikirangi te Turuki was the best-known New Zealand war leader, and is still the most difficult to understand. Settlers used to frighten their children with stories of Te Kooti. In fact he was not a madman, and he was eventually given an official pardon. He created a new religion, Ringatu, and historians have spent a lot of time trying to work out how and why he fought.

Te Kooti was one of the Rongowhakaata, from around what is now Gisborne, and fought on the government side during the war against the Pai Marire. Later, he was arrested and accused of being a spy. He was taken to Napier where he was given no trial and sent with other prisoners to the Chatham Islands.

In early 1867 he began to preach a new religion to the prisoners. Before long he had become their leader, and in early 1868 they began planning an escape. They waited until the schooner *Rifleman* arrived, seized it, then sailed back to Poverty Bay. The local magistrate, Reginald Biggs, tried to recapture Te Kooti, but Te Kooti explained that he wanted to be left alone. Biggs sent the Militia under Major Charles Westrup to chase the escaped prisoners. Te Kooti decided he would have to fight after all and ambushed the party at Paparatu.

Major Charles Westrup.

Turanganui (Gisborne) during the early 1870s.

Reginald Newton Biggs (1830?–68).

It was very embarrassing for the government. The Defence Minister, Theodore Haultain, sent Whitmore around with part of the Armed Constabulary to join the chase, but Whitmore got into a terrible argument with the Poverty Bay Militia. A few weeks later he tried to set off again, only to have an argument with the Napier Militia. Then he argued again with the Poverty Bay force. Every time he argued he sent the men who argued home, and by the time he caught up with Te Kooti in the Ruakituri River gorge, he had relatively few men left.

It was a freezing cold day, and they waded up the 'cruelly cold' river, their teeth chattering. The battle that followed left two of Whitmore's best friends dead, and the settlers were only saved from being beaten by the bravery of the kupapa chief Henare Tomoana and his Ngati Kahungunu toa. They rushed in and managed to push Te Kooti back.

Te Kooti got away to the heart of the Urewera. It was embarrassing for the government because they were also fighting Titokowaru at the same time, in Patea; it looked as if they couldn't actually organise themselves in either place.

IT'S A FACT

Colonel Whitmore's argument with the Napier Militia in July 1868 was all about food. The Militia asked for a biscuit ration. Whitmore only had flour in the stores, but he was so nasty about it that he ended up charging them with mutiny, even though he wasn't really allowed to. Then he forced them to dig their own graves. He only did it to frighten them — what he actually did was send them home in disgrace. When he got back to Turanganui he found signs welcoming 'The Gravedigger'.

38

MATAWHERO AND NGATAPA

November 1868 – January 1869

In November 1868 Te Kooti came down from the hills to attack Matawhero, his home district, just outside Turanganui (Gisborne). Te Kooti's forces killed many men, women and children, then roamed free through the district for a week, burning houses and looting.

The surviving settlers were terrified. Donald McLean wanted the kupapa to attack, but the Defence Minister, Theodore Haultain, ordered Whitmore to give up his attack on Titokowaru and come around to the East Coast with the Armed Constabulary. By Christmas Whitmore was there with more men and a Cohorn mortar, a type of gun that could fire shells high and drop them into a fort.

Te Kooti set up a fortress at Ngatapa. Rapata attacked it without success in mid-December, and a few weeks later Whitmore arrived for another go. The siege that followed lasted several days. Bad weather made it difficult for both sides, but when the clouds lifted on 4 January, Whitmore ordered Rapata's men to take the outer parapets of the pa. This meant Te Kooti could no longer get to his well. The next night Te Kooti's men lowered themselves down the cliff-side at the edge of the pa and escaped.

Rapata's men went in pursuit and caught a good number of men alive. The prisoners were brought back to Ngatapa, where Rapata's men shot many of them without trial. It was another massacre, and it was not only retribution for what Te Kooti had done at Matawhero. Rapata had been made a slave by Te Kooti's people in the 1820s, and he had never forgotten.

Ngatapa, sketched by J.C. Richmond.

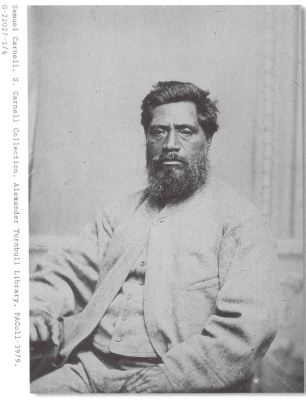

Rapata Wahawaha (?-1897), of Te Aowera, Ngati Porou.

WHAKATANE, MOHAKA AND THE UREWERA April–May 1869

Te Kooti survived the battle at Ngatapa and hid in the Urewera. Then in March 1869, with fresh followers, he launched a raid on Whakatane. Everybody was terrified by what might follow. David Balfour, who was farming near Mohaka in northern Hawke's Bay, wondered whether Te Kooti might arrive there, and remembered that he 'very rarely lay down at night without a loaded rifle for my bed mate …'

Balfour was right. A few weeks later Te Kooti did attack Mohaka, slaughtering many of the people in the pa and some of the Pakeha settlers outside, including John Lavin and his family.

Whitmore decided the only thing to do was invade the Urewera, not to attack Te Kooti but to destroy all the food supplies of the Tuhoe, who were sheltering him. Then Te Kooti would have to come out. Whitmore launched his attack in May, from

John Lavin's homestead near Mohaka. The murder of Lavin's entire family shocked settlers across New Zealand.

Alfred John Cooper, pencil, ink and watercolour Alexander Turnbull Library, A-235-012 the Whakatane side, and after a few days reached Ruatahuna. His men bashed down fences, dug up gardens, and caused mayhem. It was very hard on Tuhoe, and Te Kooti left the Urewera a few weeks later, heading for Taupo.

On the way he surprised a small group of settler militia at Opepe. There were only a few survivors from the scuffle that followed, including one man who had just washed his uniform and ended up running away without a single stitch of clothing — in the middle of winter.

Armed Constabulary at Waikaremoana, probably 1868.

Graves at Opepe, site of the 1869 ambush.

WHERE'S OPEPE TODAY?

Opepe is a patch of bush on the Napier–Taupo Road, about 17 km out of Taupo. There's a path leading to the graves of the men killed in early 1869. The battle was fought on the other side of the bush.

THE TAUPO CAMPAIGN 1869–70

The last full-scale campaign of the New Zealand Wars was fought across the Central Plateau. By this time Donald McLean was both Native and Defence Minister. John Ormond, who was in charge of the campaign, hired McDonnell to lead settler and kupapa forces against Te Kooti.

In early September 1869, McDonnell picked up the Hawke's Bay kupapa at Moawhango, on what is now the Napier–Taihape Road, and marched across the Central Plateau. Meanwhile, Henare Tomoana took another force of kupapa up the Napier–Taupo Road, and reached Turanga-o-Taupo. Here he was attacked by Te Kooti.

McDonnell assembled his own forces on one side of Lake Rotoaira, while Te Kooti's stood on the other. Te Kooti tried to tackle some of them on the Pononga Ridge, near Mount Pihanga, but was defeated and withdrew to a new redoubt at Te Porere, off to the west just above the infant Whanganui River.

The settler forces and kupapa followed him there, attacking Te Kooti and his forces at the beginning of October. It was the last full battle of the New Zealand Wars, and Te Kooti was wounded in the hand.

Henare Tomoana (?–1904).

Renata Kawepo (1808?–88), chief of Ngati Kahungunu and Ngati Te Upokoiri. Kawepo lost an eye during the battle of Te Porere when he got into a fight with the widow of Paurini. He later married her.

WHERE'S TE PORERE TODAY?

Te Porere is on State Highway 47, southwest of Turangi, on the way to the Tongariro National Park. It's signposted and has been set up as a heritage site, but there's a fair walk to get there from the carpark. The Department of Conservation keeps the place neat and tidy.

Te Porere, preserved as a historic place and maintained by the Department of Conservation.

THE END OF TE KOOTI'S WAR

After Te Porere, Te Kooti spent some time hiding in the upper Whanganui River valley. Then he went to the King Country, and in early 1870 asked for peace, but he did not want to surrender. Finally he went to Ohinemutu, near modern Rotorua, where he tried to talk to Te Arawa chiefs.

Gilbert Mair (1843-1923).

Gilbert Mair and some of the Te Arawa 'Flying Column' at Kaiteriria camp near Rotorua, after their pursuit of Te Kooti, February 1870.

The meeting was rudely interrupted by Gilbert Mair, who rushed up with his Te Arawa kupapa. Te Kooti ran off, and Mair charged after him across hill and dale, towards the Urewera. Mair was so eager to catch his enemy that he outran his own men and ended up facing Te Kooti's right-hand-man, Peka Makarini, alone. In the fight that followed he shot Peka Makarini, only to be bitten by Makarini's dog. Te Kooti escaped again.

Donald McLean decided to send Te Arawa and other kupapa into the Urewera. For the next three years Maori forces chased Te Kooti, but they never caught him. Finally, early in 1872, he was found near Lake Waikaremoana. There was a short battle, which Te Kooti lost. He went to the King Country, where Tawhaio gave him sanctuary.

WHO WAS PEKA MAKARINI?

Peka Makarini's mother was Maori, but his father was said to be an important settler official. It was rumoured his father was Donald McLean, but nobody could prove it. What they did know was that Peka Makarini could read and write English. He could also play the bugle, and used one captured in the Chatham Islands to annoy settler forces when they were within hearing by playing the tunes that usually called them to their meals.

People of Parihaka pose for the camera, 1880s.

PEACE WITH THE KING COUNTRY, 1881—83

Settlers and Maori stopped shooting at each other when Te Kooti's war ended in 1872, but the reasons they had been fighting were still apparent. Both sides looked for different ways of solving the problem.

Maori decided to use politics and law, and the new battlefield became Parliament and the courts. Ngati Kahungunu started taking legal action over land deals in Hawke's Bay. Their chief, Karaitiana Takamoana, also entered Parliament.

In Taranaki the prophet Te Whiti o te Rongomai tried another idea. He set up the village of Parihaka and declared he would oppose the settlers, but never fight. Settler authorities couldn't understand this. In 1881 they sent the Armed Constabulary to arrest Te Whiti, but he hadn't actually done anything, and in 1883 he was released from prison. Parihaka became a very famous and important place for Maori, and still is today.

The Armed Constabulary waiting to advance on Parihaka, November 1881.

45

Officials gather to turn the first sod on the Main Trunk Line at Puniu, 1884.

Daniel Manders Beere, D.M. Beere Collection, Alexander Turnbull Library, PAColl-3081, G-96175-1/2

In 1881 both Tawhaio and Rewi Maniapoto made official peace, eventually making it possible for the government to pardon many Maori who had fought, including Te Kooti. But the King Country was still separate, and that was a problem for the government. This was solved very cleverly by putting the Main Trunk Line straight through the whole region. What this meant was that hundreds of railway builders, their wives and their children all moved into the King Country. When the train came, it brought more people and trade. So the King Country was drawn into New Zealand, whether Tawhaio liked it or not.

46

THE WAR AND HISTORIANS

Somebody once said that historians never finish arguing. And that's true. We know *what* happened, but knowing *what* happened doesn't always tell us *why* things happened, and everybody has different ideas.

For many years after the wars it was said that Maori and settler had fought, made up, and become friends. It was also said that the British and settlers had beaten Maori. The best book of this sort was written in the 1920s by James Cowan, who went to all the battle sites and talked to a lot of the old soldiers.

That's how everybody saw the wars for years. Then in the early 1980s, historian James Belich came up with a new idea. He said that Maori had done better than we thought, and that the wars hadn't solved New Zealand's race relations problems. He also came up with some new military ideas. Belich's new theory about the military side of the wars was rejected by some military historians. But new ideas are what history is all about, and we can expect other new ideas to surface as time goes on. That's what makes history, and the New Zealand Wars, so interesting.

SELECTED FURTHER READING

Belich, James, *The New Zealand Wars*, Penguin, Auckland 1986.

Binney, Judith, *Redemption Songs*, Auckland University Press/Bridget Williams Books, Auckland 1996.

Cowan, James, *The New Zealand Wars, Volume 1: 1845–64*, Government Printer, Wellington 1922.

Cowan, James, *The New Zealand Wars, Volume 2: The Hauhau Wars*, Government Print, Wellington 1923.

Wilson, Ormond, *War in the Tussock*, Government Printer/Historic Places Trust, Wellington 1961.

Wright, Matthew, *The Reed Illustrated History of New Zealand*, Reed, Auckland 2004.

Wright, Matthew, *Two Peoples, One Land: the New Zealand Wars*, Reed, Auckland 2006.

INDEX

Ahuriri 32
Anaua, Hori Kingi te 29
Auckland 6, 9, 22, 26

Balfour, David 40
Bates, Lieutenant H.S. 19
Bay of Islands 5, 9, 11
Bay of Plenty 5, 31
Biggs, Reginald Newton 37, 38
Boulcott (settler) 12
Boulcott's Farm 14
Broughton, Charles 30
Busby, James 7

Cameron Road 26
Cameron, Lieutenant-General Sir Duncan 20, 21, 22, 23, 26, 27, 28, 36
Carey, Brigadier-General George 23
Central Plateau 5, 42
Chatham Islands 31, 37
Cracroft, Captain Peter 16, 17

Despard, Colonel Henry 10

East Cape 31, 32, 35, 39

FitzRoy, Robert 8, 9, 11

Gate Pa see Pukehinahina
Gillfillian, J.A. 13
Gisborne 6, 35, 37
Gold, Colonel E.C. 16, 17
Gore-Browne, Governor Thomas Robert 18
Great South Road (Auckland) 5
Great South Road 21
Greer, Colonel 26
Grey, Governor George 11, 12, 13, 20, 26, 29

Hamilton 5
Hamilton, Captain 27
Hapaurona 16, 18
Haratua, Te 9
Haultain, Defence Minister Theodore 35, 38, 39
Haumene, Te Ua 29, 30
Hawke's Bay 5, 32, 36, 40, 42, 45
Heaphy, Charles 25
Heke, Hone see Pokai, Hone Wiremu Heke
Hirst, Grace 28
Hobson, Captain William 7, 8, 9
Horokiwi 28
Horowhenua 13
Huia Fort 28
Huirama, Te 21
Huirangi 18
Hulme, Lieutenant-Colonel William 10, 12
Hunter, William 34
Hutt River 12
Hutt Valley 5, 12

Kaipopo pa 17
Kawepo, Renata 6, 42
Kawiti, Te Ruki 9, 10, 11, 17
Keepa, Te 30, 37
Kikihiki 18
King Country 5, 16, 17, 21, 44, 45, 46
Kingi, Wiremu (King, William) 16
Kororareka (Russell) 9

Lake Omapere 10
Lake Rotoaira 42
Lake Waikare 22
Lake Waikaremoana 44
Lloyd, Captain T.W.J. 30

Mahoetahi Hill 17, 19
Mair, Gilbert 31, 44
Mair, William 22, 23, 31
Makarini, Peka 44, 45
Mamaku, Hemi Topine te 12, 13
Mangapiko River 25
Mangatawhiri River 21
Maniapoto, Rewi Manga 15, 21, 22, 25, 24, 46
Maramarua 21
Matai-taua pa 13
Matawhero 39
Maungatautari 23
McDonnell, Lieutenant-Colonel Thomas 34, 35, 42
McKillop, Midshipman H. 28
McLean, Donald 13, 31, 32, 39, 42, 44
McNeill, Lieutenant-Colonel 25
Mercer 21
Meremere 21, 22
Moawhango 42
Mohaka 40
Molesworth's Farm 12
Monmouth Redoubt 27
Moturoa 35, 36
Mould, Colonel 22
Mount Pihanga 42

Napier 6, 32, 36, 37
Nene, Tamati Waka 9, 10, 11
New Plymouth 6, 8, 15, 17, 18, 35
Nga Puhi 9, 11
Ngai te Rangi 26
Ngaruawahia 21, 22
Ngatapa 39, 40
Ngati Haua 15, 17
Ngati Hineuru 32
Ngati Kahungunu 32, 38, 42, 45
Ngati Mahuta 21
Ngati Maniapoto 23
Ngati Paoa 21
Ngati Rangitahi 12
Ngati Raukawa 23
Ngati Ruahine 34
Ngati Ruanui 17
Ngati Tama 12

Ngati Te Upokoiri 42
Ngati Toa 12
Nukumaru 35

Ohaeawai 10, 28
Ohinemutu 44
Omarunui 32, 33
Opepe 41
Opotiki 31
Orakau 23, 29
Ormond, John 42
Otautu 35

Paekakariki 13
Parihaka 45
Patea 35
Patea 38
Paterangi 23, 25
Pauahatanui 13
Pehiatu pa 30
Petane (Bay View) 32
Pikopiko 23
Pokai, Hone Wiremu Heke (Hone Heke) 9, 10, 11
Pononga Ridge 42
Poroutawhao 13
Poverty Bay 5
Pratt, Major-General Thomas 17, 18
Pratt's Sap 19
Pukehinahina (Gate Pa) 5, 26
Pukerangiora 18, 19
Puketutu 10
Puniu 23
Punui River 23

Rangihaeata, Te 12, 13, 14
Rangiriri 22, 24
Rangitake, Te 16, 17, 18
Rangitaki, Te 16
Rangitauia, Matene te 29
Rapata 39
Rau, Kereropa te 31
Rauparaha, Te 12, 13
Richardson, J.C. 30
Rongomai, Te Whiti o te 45
Rongowhakaata 37
Rotorua 44
Ruakituri River 38
Ruapekapeka pa 11
Ruaruru 34
Ruatahuna 41

Sentry Hill 29
Shortland, Willoughby 8

Taiporutu, Te Wetini 17
Takamoana, Karaitiana 45
Tamihana, Wiremu (Thompson, William) see Tarapipipi, Te Waharoa
Taranaki pa 19
Taranaki 5, 8, 15, 28, 29, 31, 34, 45
Tarapipipi, Te Waharoa 15, 23

Taupo 23, 41
Tauranga 26
Tauranga-ika pa 35
Tawhaio 44, 46
Te Ahuahu 29, 30
Te Arawa 31, 44
Te Arei 18, 19
Te Atiawa 13, 16, 18, 35
Te Awamutu 23
Te Haroto 32
Te Keepa 35
Te Kohia 16
Te Kooti see Turuki, Te Kooti
Te Ngutu o te Manu (The Beak of the Bird) 34, 35
Te Porere 42, 43, 44
Titokowaru 30, 34, 35, 39
Tomoana, Henare 6, 38, 42
Tonganui, Hauraki 23
Treaty of Waitangi 7, 9, 15
Tuaia, Rawiri 26
Tuhoe 40, 41
Turanganui (Gisborne) 31, 35, 39
Turanga-o-Taupo 42
Turuki, Te Kooti Arikiriangi te 28, 30, 37, 38, 39, 40,41, 42, 44, 45, 46
Turuturumokai 34
Tutaekuri River 32

Urewera 5, 23, 31, 38, 40, 41, 44

Volkner, Carl Sylvius 3231
Von Tempsky, Gustavus Ferdinand 21, 35
Vosper, Private 25

Waerenga-a-hika pa 31
Wahawaha, Rapata 6, 31, 39
Waikare Swamp 22
Waikato 5, 15, 18, 20, 22, 23, 28
Waikato River 21, 22
Waipa River 23
Wairoa 35
Waitangi 9
Waitara 15, 16, 17, 18
Waitotara 30
Waitotara River 18
Wakefield, Edward Gibbon 7, 8, 12
Wanganui (Petrie) 8, 13, 29
Weld, Premier Frederick 29
Wellington 5, 8, 12, 28, 35
Westrup, Major Charles 37
Wetini, Te 18
Whakatane 40
Whanganui 12
Whanganui River 42, 44
Wherowhero, Te 15
White, John 29
Whitmore, Lieutenant-Colonel George S. 28, 30, 32, 35, 36, 38, 39, 40